THE SLIM 800 HOT AIR FRYER

Simply Quick & Fast Food

THE SLIM 800 HOT AIR FRYER SIMPLY QUICK & FAST FOOD

978-1-913005-50-4

DISCLAIMER

This book is designed to provide information on meals & snacks that can be made using an electric hot air fryer appliance. Some recipes may contain nuts or traces of nuts. Those suffering from any allergies associated with nuts should avoid any recipes containing nuts or nut based oils. This information is provided and sold with the knowledge that the publisher and author do not offer any legal or other professional advice. In the case of a need for any such expertise consult with the appropriate professional.

This book does not contain all information available on the subject, and other sources of recipes are available.
Every effort has been made to make this book as accurate as possible. However, there may be typographical and or content errors. Therefore, this book should serve only as a general guide and not as the ultimate source of subject information.

This book contains information that might be dated and is intended only to educate and entertain.
The author and publisher shall have no liability or responsibility to any person or entity regarding any loss or damage incurred, or alleged to have incurred, directly or indirectly, by the information contained in this book.

CONTENTS

INTRODUCTION 8

POULTRY 11

Chicken & Rice Bake 12
Chicken Fried Rice 13
Chicken Thighs with Green Beans 14
Turkey & Roasted Broccoli 15
Chicken with Honey Sprouts 16
Almond Chicken 17
Chicken Meatballs 18
Chicken Kofta 19
Parmesan Crusted Chicken 20
Chicken & Sweetcorn Bowl 21
Crispy Cashew Chicken 22
Zesty Coconut Chicken 23
Coriander Chicken 24
Spiced Parma Thighs 25
Mediterranean Chicken 26
Chicken & Peppers 27
Chicken & Asparagus Five Spice 28
Ginger Fire Wings 29
Sweet Soy Drummers 30
Simply Crispy Wings 31
Chicken & Olives 32

MEAT 33

Honey Glazed Gammon 34
Pork Burgers 35
Pork Chops & Baby Potatoes 36

Spiced Lamb Stir-Fry 37
Thai Pork 38
Pork Tenderloin & Apple 39
Beef, Beans & Rice 40
Sausage Gnocchi 41
Garlic Beef & Beansprouts 42
Cheese-Stuffed Meatballs 43
Lamb 'Kebab' Pittas 44
Moroccan Lamb 45
Steak & Broccoli Stir-Fry 46
Cocoa Beef 47
Beef Keema 48
Beef & Chickpea Stew 49
Rich Ragu 50
Steak & White Bean Bake 51
Spanish Fried Rice 52
Chinese Pork & Cabbage 53
Balsamic Beef & Potatoes 54

FISH & SEAFOOD **55**
Sesame Tuna Steaks 56
Haddock with Sweet Potato Wedges 57
Coconut Prawns with Mango Salsa 58
Fish & Green Beans 59
Salmon with Asparagus 60
Scallop Rice-Bowl 61
Chorizo & King Prawn Wraps 62
Super Simple Sweet & Sour 63
Garlic Prawns with Sautéed Peppers 64
Thai Prawn Stir Fry 65
Salt & Pepper Prawns with Veggies 66
Crispy Garlic Prawns 67
Fried Squid Rings 68

VEGETABLES & SIDE DISHES 69

Balsamic Roasted Vegetables 70
Anchovy Broccoli with Chilli 71
Mustard Potatoes with Spinach 72
Ginger Cabbage & Peas 73
Honey-Glazed Baby Carrots 74
Lemon Garlic Green Beans 75
Spiced Sweet Potato Wedges 76
Roasted Beetroot & Feta 77
Garlic Butter Asparagus 78
Herb-Crusted Cauliflower 79
Lemon Herb Courgette 80
Teriyaki Tofu & Broccoli 81
Spicy Tofu Stir-Fry 82
Garlic Rosemary Chickpeas 83
Thyme Roasted Root Veg 84

WHOLEFOOD SNACKS 85

Cinnamon Apple Chips / Air-Fried Pineapple Rings 86
Crispy Banana Chips / Honey-Glazed Pear Slices 87
Roasted Strawberries / Spiced Peach Halves 88
Baked Grapefruit / Crispy Kiwi Chips 89
Air-Fried Mango Slices / Caramelized Plums 90
Crispy Kale Chips / Sweet Potato Fries 91
Courgette Chips / Parsnip Crisps 92
Spiced Carrot Fries / Butternut Squash Bites 93
Spicy Chickpeas / Garlic Mushrooms 94
Brussels Sprouts Chips / Broccoli Bites 95

INTRODUCTION

What is the Slim '800' Lifestyle ?

The Slim 800 Diet is an effort to return to a healthier way of eating that emphasises fasting and balanced nutrition. Fasting is probably most well-known as the 5:2 Diet—a great and flexible way to approach weight loss and less restrictive than many other diets. The 5:2 approach means you can eat 'normally' for 5 days a week and fast for 2. It's revolutionised the way people think about dieting.

By allowing you the freedom to eat normally for MOST of the week and fast by restricting your calorie intake for just TWO non-consecutive days a week (800 calories per day for men and women), you keep yourself motivated and remove that dreaded feeling of constantly denying yourself the food you really want to eat. It still takes willpower, but it's nowhere near as much of a grind when you know that you have tomorrow to look forward to. It's all about freedom. The ability to be flexible with the days you choose to fast makes the likelihood of you sticking to the diet for a prolonged period, or even indefinitely as a lifestyle choice, much higher than a regime that requires calorie restriction every single day.

With The Slim 800: Hot Air Fryer Simply Quick & Fast Food, we've given you lots of air fryer recipe ideas which you'll be able to use on your fast days and on your 'normal' days. Everything is calorie counted with nutritional breakdown so you'll be able to keep things on track more easily.

Your ultimate guide to healthier frying.

Hot air fryers are revolutionizing the way we cook, becoming an indispensable addition to the modern kitchen. Once you experience the convenience and health benefits of a hot air fryer, you'll wonder how you ever lived without one!

A hot air fryer allows you to create quick, easy, and healthy meals with just a fraction of the oil required by traditional frying methods. There's no need for preheating or mixing, and it can cook a wide variety of dishes, from snacks to main courses—not just chips! Speaking of which, air-fried chips deserve a special mention for their crispy perfection achieved with minimal oil, making them a healthier option.

The Slim 800: Hot Air Fryer Simply Quick & Fast Food is your ultimate guide to healthier frying. It features a diverse collection of recipes, including starters, main courses and sides. Whether you're preparing a family meal, hosting a party, or indulging in a snack, this cookbook has you covered. It's the only hot air fryer recipe book you'll ever need!

Simple, Quick, Convenient, and Nutritious

This book is designed for those who value simplicity and convenience without sacrificing nutrition. Whether you're on a busy schedule or just looking to make healthier choices, the recipes in this book are crafted to be quick, easy, and nutritious—perfect for anyone who wants to eat well without spending hours in the kitchen.

HOW DOES HOT AIR FRYING WORK?

Unlike traditional deep frying, a hot air fryer uses very hot air (up to 200°C) to circulate around the food, cooking it quickly with a crispy outer layer.

TEMPERATURE CONTROL

Most air fryers come with adjustable temperature controls and timers. If yours doesn't, it's likely preset to cook at 200°C/400°F. Keep an eye on cooking times to ensure perfect results.

We use fresh, inexpensive, lower-calorie and lower-fat ingredients, all readily available at your local supermarket.

HOW CAN IT FRY WITH SO LITTLE OIL?

The efficient hot air circulation requires only a minimal amount of oil. Often, a light spray of oil is enough, making it the healthiest way to fry. Choose your preferred low-calorie spray oil, whether it's olive, coconut, or sunflower oil.

DOES HOT AIR FRIED FRIED FOOD TASTE DIFFERENT?

Hot air fried food often tastes better than traditional fried food. The reduced fat content doesn't compromise flavour, and the method preserves the natural taste of your ingredients.

CLEANER, SAFER, HEALTHIER

Hot air fryers use significantly less oil—often just a spoonful—making them a healthier option compared to traditional deep fryers. They use fresh oil for each cooking session, eliminating strong odours and smoke. This method is not only healthier but also safer, with most fryers pausing the cooking process when the lid is lifted.

OUR RECIPES

Reflecting the simplicity of hot air frying, our recipes are easy to follow with minimal preparation and cooking times. We use fresh, inexpensive, lower-calorie and lower-fat ingredients, all readily available at your local supermarket. Each recipe includes calorie counts and nutritional information, perfect for those following an 800-calorie fasting day. We minimise the use of store cupboard ingredients to keep your store cupboard streamlined and your cooking affordable. Some recipes serve four, and given that air fryer capacities vary, you might need to adjust cooking times for batch cooking.

TIPS

To get the best results from your hot air fryer, keep these tips in mind:

- Remove food promptly once cooking is complete to maintain crispiness.
- Clean your appliance after each use; most parts are dishwasher safe.
- Avoid abrasive cleaning materials to protect the non-stick coating.
- Ensure food has plenty of space in the fryer for even cooking.
- Read the manufacturer's instructions thoroughly to understand your fryer's functions and maintain the warranty.
- Air fryers vary in capacity; you may need to cook in batches.
- Preheat your air fryer before adding food.
- Cooking times are guidelines; check your food to ensure it's thoroughly cooked before serving.

Once you experience the convenience and health benefits of a hot air fryer, you'll wonder how you ever lived without one!

POULTRY

CHICKEN & RICE BAKE

Serves 4

INGREDIENTS

- 1 onion, finely chopped
- 2 garlic cloves, minced
- 1 courgette, chopped
- 1 red pepper, chopped
- 100g pitted olives, halved
- 200g leftover cooked chicken, shredded
- 500g pre-cooked brown rice
- 2 eggs, beaten
- 1 tbsp each tomato puree, dried oregano, basil & smoked paprika
- 1 lemon, juiced and zested
- 30g reduced-fat feta cheese, crumbled
- 1 tbsp olive oil
- Low-calorie spray oil
- Salt & pepper to taste
- 2 tbsp fresh basil, chopped

NUTRITION

- Calories: 320
- Protein: 18g
- Total Fat: 12g
- Saturated Fat: 3g
- Carbs: 34g
- Fibre: 5g
- Sugars: 4g

METHOD

1 In a large bowl, combine the chopped onion, garlic, courgette, and pepper. Season with salt, pepper, oregano, basil, and smoked paprika. Spray with low-calorie oil. Place the mixture in an air fryer-safe dish and cook at 180°C (350°F) for 8-10 minutes, stirring halfway through, until the vegetables are softened.

2 Add the shredded chicken, pre-cooked brown rice, tomato puree, lemon zest, lemon juice, and beaten eggs to the dish. Stir to combine everything evenly.

3 Return the dish to the air fryer and cook for an additional 7-9 minutes at 180°C (350°F), stirring occasionally to ensure even cooking and that the eggs are fully set.

4 Once the bake is cooked through, remove from the air fryer and stir in the olives. Sprinkle with reduced-fat crumbled feta cheese on top. Garnish with fresh basil and serve.

CHICKEN FRIED RICE

Serves 4

INGREDIENTS

- 1 onion, chopped
- 2 garlic cloves, crushed
- 125g frozen peas
- 125g mushrooms, chopped
- 200g left-over cooked chicken, shredded
- 1 tsp Chinese Five Spice powder
- 500g pre-cooked brown rice
- 2 eggs, beaten
- 1 tbsp soy sauce
- 2 tbsp freshly chopped flat-leaf parsley
- Low-calorie spray oil
- Salt & pepper to taste

NUTRITION

- Calories: 355
- Protein: 20g
- Total Fat: 9g
- Saturated Fat: 2g
- Carbs: 45g
- Fibre: 4g
- Sugars: 3g

METHOD

1 In a large bowl, combine the onion, garlic, peas and mushroom. Season and spray with low-calorie oil. Place in an air fryer-safe dish and cook at 180°C (350°F) for 8-10 minutes, stirring halfway through, until the vegetables are softened.

2 Add the cooked chicken, Chinese Five Spice powder, and pre-cooked brown rice to the dish. Pour the beaten eggs over the rice mixture and combine. Place the dish back in the air fryer and continue for an additional 7-9 minutes, stirring occasionally to ensure even cooking and that the eggs are fully set.

3 Stir in the soy sauce, adjust seasoning sprinkle with chopped parsley and serve.

CHICKEN THIGHS WITH GREEN BEANS

Serves 4

INGREDIENTS

- 4 skinless bone-in chicken thighs
- 300g green beans, trimmed
- 1 tsp garlic powder
- 1 tsp dried basil
- 1 tsp dried oregano
- 2 tbsp grated Parmesan cheese
- Low-calorie spray oil
- Salt & pepper to taste
- Lemon wedges for serving

NUTRITION

- Calories: 290
- Protein: 27g
- Total Fat: 17g
- Saturated Fat: 5g
- Carbs: 6g
- Fibre: 2g
- Sugars: 2g

METHOD

1 Spray the green beans with oil. Season and sprinkle with garlic powder. Add to the air fryer basket and cook at 180°C (350°F) for 7 minutes.

2 While the green beans are cooking, season the chicken thighs, spray with oil and combine with dried basil, oregano, salt, and pepper.

3 Add the chicken to the air fryer basket and cook at 180°C (350°F) for an additional 15-18 minutes, or until the chicken is cooked through.

4 In the last 3 minutes of cooking, sprinkle the Parmesan cheese over the chicken and green beans. Continue cooking until the cheese is melted and slightly crispy. Serve with lemon wedges on the side.

TURKEY & ROASTED BROCCOLI

Serves 4

INGREDIENTS

- 4 small turkey fillets
- 1 head of broccoli, cut into florets
- 1 tsp garlic powder
- 2 tbsp olive oil
- 1 tsp dried thyme
- 1 tsp dried oregano
- 1 lemon (zest and juice)
- Salt & pepper to taste
- 2 tbsp freshly chopped parsley

NUTRITION

- Calories: 392
- Protein: 23g
- Total Fat: 15g
- Saturated Fat: 7g
- Carbs: 42g
- Fibre: 2.5g
- Sugars: 4g

METHOD

1 In a large bowl, combine the broccoli with the garlic, 1 tbsp olive oil, salt, and pepper. Add to the air fryer basket and cook at 180°C (350°F) for 3 minutes.

2 While the broccoli is cooking, season the turkey fillets with thyme, oregano, lemon zest, and the remaining olive oil.

3 After the broccoli has cooked for 3 minutes, add the seasoned turkey fillets to the air fryer basket. Continue cooking for an additional 14-18 minutes, or until the turkey is cooked through and piping hot.

4 Drizzle with fresh lemon juice, sprinkle with chopped parsley and serve.

CHICKEN WITH HONEY SPROUTS

Serves 4

INGREDIENTS

- 2 onions, sliced
- 300g Brussels sprouts, halved
- 2 tsp garlic powder
- 4 small chicken fillets
- ½ tsp each of salt, cumin & turmeric
- 2 tbsp honey
- 1 tbsp balsamic vinegar
- 2 tbsp freshly chopped flat-leaf parsley
- Low-calorie spray oil
- Salt & pepper to taste

NUTRITION

- Calories: 310
- Protein: 28g
- Total Fat: 7g
- Saturated Fat: 1.5g
- Carbs: 28g
- Fibre: 4g
- Sugars: 14g

METHOD

1 Place the onions, Brussels sprouts and garlic powder in a large bowl. Spray with oil, season with salt and pepper, and combine. Add to the air fryer basket and cook at 180°C (350°F) for 10 minutes.

2 While the vegetables are cooking, season the chicken fillets with salt, cumin, and turmeric. Lightly spray with oil.

3 After the vegetables have cooked for 10 minutes, add the seasoned chicken fillets to the air fryer basket. In a small bowl, mix the honey with balsamic vinegar and drizzle over the chicken and Brussels sprouts.

4 4. Cook for an additional 18-22 minutes at 180°C (350°F) or until the chicken is cooked through and piping hot. Sprinkle with parsley and serve.

ALMOND CHICKEN

Serves 4

INGREDIENTS

- 2 tsp garlic powder
- 2 onions, sliced
- 1 tbsp mild curry powder
- ½ tsp salt
- 1 tbsp tomato puree
- 2 tbsp ground almonds
- 500g chicken breast, cubed
- 3 tbsp fat-free Greek yoghurt
- Low-calorie spray oil
- Salt & pepper to taste

NUTRITION

- Calories: 290
- Protein: 34g
- Total Fat: 10g
- Saturated Fat: 1.5g
- Carbs: 9g
- Fibre: 3g
- Sugars: 4g

METHOD

1 Place the garlic and onions in the air fryer basket with a few sprays of low-calorie oil. Cook at 180°C (350°F) for 5 minutes until the onions soften.

2 In a bowl combine together the curry powder, salt, tomato puree, ground almonds, and cubed chicken breast. Spray with oil, add to the air fryer and continue cooking at 180°C (350°F) for 14-16 minutes, until the chicken is fully cooked through.

3 Once the chicken is done, remove the air fryer basket and stir in the Greek yoghurt. Mix until the dish is creamy and well combined.

4 Adjust seasoning and serve.

CHICKEN MEATBALLS

Serves 4

INGREDIENTS

- 500g chicken mince
- 2 garlic cloves, crushed
- 2 tbsp fresh breadcrumbs
- ½ tsp each mixed herbs, paprika, brown sugar & salt
- 2 tbsp sundried tomato puree/paste
- 3 red or yellow peppers, sliced
- Low-calorie spray oil
- Salt & pepper to taste

NUTRITION

- Calories: 260
- Protein: 27g
- Total Fat: 10g
- Saturated Fat: 2g
- Carbs: 12g
- Fibre: 2g
- Sugars: 4g

METHOD

1 Put the chicken mince, garlic cloves, breadcrumbs, dried spices, sugar, salt and sundried tomato puree in a food processor and pulse a few times until combined.

2 Take the mixture out and form into 12-15 small meatballs with your hands.

3 Season the peppers, spray with oil and place in in the air fryer basket to cook at 180°C (350°F) for 10 minutes.

4 Add the chicken meatballs and cook for a further 10-15 minutes or until the meatballs are cooked through.

5 Check the seasoning and serve.

CHICKEN KOFTA

Serves 4

INGREDIENTS

- 500g chicken mince
- 2 garlic cloves, crushed
- 2 tbsp fresh breadcrumbs
- ½ tsp each ground turmeric, coriander, paprika, brown sugar & salt
- 400g potatoes, peeled & cubed
- 100g spinach leaves
- 4 tbsp fat free Greek yoghurt
- Lemon wedges to serve
- Low-calorie spray oil
- Salt & pepper to taste

NUTRITION

- Calories: 315
- Protein: 29g
- Total Fat: 10g
- Saturated Fat: 2g
- Carbs: 28g
- Fibre: 4g
- Sugars: 3g

METHOD

1 Put the chicken mince, garlic cloves, breadcrumbs, dried spices, sugar & salt in a food processor and pulse a few times until combined.

2 Take the mixture out and form into 12-15 small meatballs with your hands.

3 Season the potatoes, spray with oil and place in in the air fryer basket to cook at 180°C (350°F) for 15 minutes.

4 Add the chicken meatballs & and cook for a further 20 minutes or until the meatballs are cooked through.

5 Add the spinach and cook for 5 minutes or until the spinach begins to wilt.

6 Season and serve with a dollop of Greek yoghurt and lemon wedges.

PARMESAN CRUSTED CHICKEN

Serves 4

INGREDIENTS

- 1 onion, sliced
- 200g mushrooms, sliced
- 1 pepper, sliced
- 1 courgette, sliced
- 2 tsp olive oil
- 1 tsp dried rosemary
- 500g/1lb 2oz skinless chicken breast, cubed
- 1 tsp garlic powder
- 1 tsp paprika
- 50g grated Parmesan cheese
- Salt & pepper to taste

NUTRITION

- Calories: 320
- Protein: 36g
- Total Fat: 13g
- Saturated Fat: 4g
- Carbs: 10g
- Fibre: 3g
- Sugars: 5g

METHOD

1 In a large bowl add the sliced onions, mushrooms, pepper, and courgette. Drizzle with olive oil, season with salt and pepper, and combine.

2 Transfer the vegetable mixture to the air fryer basket and cook for 7-8 minutes at 180°C (350°F) shaking the basket halfway through.

3 While the vegetables are cooking, combine the cubed chicken breast with the rosemary, garlic powder, paprika, salt, and pepper until evenly coated.

4 Add the chicken to the air fryer basket and cook everything together at 180°C (350°F) for an additional 12-15 minutes.

5 In the last 2-3 minutes of cooking, open the air fryer and sprinkle the grated Parmesan cheese evenly over the chicken and vegetables. Continue cooking until the Parmesan has melted and formed a slight crust. Make sure the chicken is cooked through and the vegetables are tender before serving.

CHICKEN & SWEETCORN BOWL

Serves 4

INGREDIENTS

- 500g skinless chicken breast, cubed
- 1 tbsp cornflour
- 1 tsp garlic powder
- 1 tsp paprika
- 2 sweet peppers, sliced
- 1 onion, sliced
- 125g frozen sweetcorn
- 3 medium carrots, sliced into thin batons
- Low-calorie spray oil
- Salt & pepper to taste

NUTRITION

- Calories: 240
- Protein: 28g
- Total Fat: 3g
- Saturated Fat: 1g
- Carbs: 24g
- Fibre: 5g
- Sugars: 7g

METHOD

1 Toss the cubed chicken breast with the cornflour, garlic powder, paprika, salt, and pepper in a large bowl, ensuring the chicken is evenly coated.

2 Add the sliced peppers, onion, frozen sweetcorn, and carrot batons to the bowl. Mix everything together until the vegetables are well coated with the seasoning.

3 Lightly spray with low-calorie spray oil. Place the seasoned chicken and vegetable mixture into the air fryer basket.

4 Cook at 180°C (350°F) for 15-18 minutes, shaking the basket or stirring the contents halfway through to ensure even cooking. Make sure the chicken is cooked through and the vegetables are tender before serving.

CRISPY CASHEW CHICKEN

Serves 4

INGREDIENTS

- 500g skinless chicken breast, cubed
- 1 egg, beaten
- 2 tbsp cornflour
- 100g cashew nuts, (Use a rolling pin to bash into a fine crumb)
- 1 tsp garlic powder
- 1 tsp paprika
- 2 onions, sliced
- 2 tbsp freshly chopped coriander
- Low-calorie spray oil
- Salt & pepper to taste

NUTRITION

- Calories: 365
- Protein: 32g
- Total Fat: 16g
- Saturated Fat: 3g
- Carbs: 18g
- Fibre: 2g
- Sugars: 4g

METHOD

1 Dip the chicken and onions in the beaten egg.

2 Combine the cornflour, cashew crumbs, garlic powder and paprika.

3 Use this cashew flour to coat the chicken and onions and spay with some low-calorie oil.

4 Place in in the air fryer basket and cook at 180°C (350°F) for 14-16 minutes, shaking the basket or stirring the contents halfway through.

5 Once the chicken is cooked through and piping hot, sprinkle with the freshly chopped coriander and serve.

ZESTY COCONUT CHICKEN

Serves 4

INGREDIENTS

- 1 tsp garlic powder
- ½ tsp ground cumin
- ½ tsp ground ginger
- 1 tsp paprika
- 1 tbsp desiccated coconut
- 1 tbsp olive oil
- 1 tbsp lemon juice
- 500g/1lb 2oz skinless chicken breast, cubed
- 1 onion, sliced
- 200g cherry tomatoes, halved
- Salt & pepper to taste
- 2 tbsp freshly chopped flat-leaf parsley

NUTRITION

- Calories: 290
- Protein: 30g
- Total Fat: 13g
- Saturated Fat: 4g
- Carbs: 9g
- Fibre: 2g
- Sugars: 4g

METHOD

1 Combine the garlic, cumin, ground ginger, paprika, desiccated coconut, olive oil and lemon juice with some salt and pepper in a large bowl.

2 Add the chicken and toss to coat the chicken evenly with the spice mixture. Allow it to marinate for at least 15 minutes (or up to 2 hours in the fridge).

3 Add the sliced onion and halved cherry tomatoes to the bowl and toss everything together until the vegetables are well coated with the marinade.

4 Place the marinated chicken and vegetable mixture into the air fryer basket. Cook at 180°C for 14-16 minutes, shaking the basket or stirring the contents halfway through.

5 Once the chicken is cooked through and piping hot sprinkle with the freshly chopped flat-leaf parsley and serve.

CORIANDER CHICKEN

Serves 4

INGREDIENTS

- 500g skinless chicken breast, cubed
- 1 red onion, sliced
- 1 tsp garlic powder
- 1 tsp ground coriander
- ½ tsp each ground cumin & salt
- 2 tbsp freshly chopped coriander
- Low-calorie spray oil
- Salt & pepper to taste

NUTRITION

- Calories: 220
- Protein: 33g
- Total Fat: 5g
- Saturated Fat: 1g
- Carbs: 5g
- Fibre: 1g
- Sugars: 2g

METHOD

1 Toss the chicken and onions in the dry spices.

2 Give the seasoned ingredients a light spray of oil and place in the basket of the air fryer.

3 Cook at 180°C (350°F) for 12-14 minutes, shaking the basket halfway through.

4 Make sure the chicken is cooked through and piping hot. Sprinkle over the chopped coriander and serve.

SPICED PARMA THIGHS

Serves 4

INGREDIENTS

- 1 tsp garlic powder
- ½ tsp each cumin, salt, paprika & cayenne pepper
- 40g Parmesan cheese, grated
- 12 bone-in, skinless chicken thighs
- Low-calorie spray oil
- Salt & pepper to taste

NUTRITION

- Calories: 370
- Protein: 36g
- Total Fat: 24g
- Saturated Fat: 7g
- Carbs: 2g
- Fibre: 0g
- Sugars: 0g

METHOD

1 Combine all the dry ingredients and grated cheese together.

2 Carefully this onto the chicken thighs.

3 Give the chicken a light spray of oil and place in the basket of the air fryer, sprinkling on any left-over cheese.

4 Cook at 180°C (350°F) for 12-14 minutes, shaking the basket halfway through.

5 Make sure the chicken is cooked through and piping hot. Season and serve.

MEDITERRANEAN CHICKEN

Serves 4

INGREDIENTS

- 500g skinless chicken breast, cubed
- 50g (jarred) sundried tomatoes
- 50g olives, halved
- 1 onion, sliced
- 1 tsp garlic powder
- 2 tsp dried basil
- Low-calorie spray oil
- Salt & pepper to taste

NUTRITION

- Calories: 250
- Protein: 31g
- Total Fat: 10g
- Saturated Fat: 2g
- Carbs: 6g
- Fibre: 2g
- Sugars: 3g

METHOD

1 Toss the chicken, sundried tomatoes, olives and onions in the herbs.

2 Give the seasoned ingredients a light spray of oil and place in the basket of the air fryer.

3 Cook at 180°C (350°F) for 12-14 minutes, shaking the basket or stirring the contents halfway through.

4 Make sure the chicken is cooked through and piping hot. Season and serve.

CHICKEN & PEPPERS

Serves 4

INGREDIENTS

- 1 red pepper, sliced
- 1 yellow pepper, sliced
- 1 red onion, sliced
- 500g skinless chicken breast, sliced
- 200g cherry tomatoes, halved
- 1 tsp cayenne pepper
- ½ tsp cumin
- 1 tsp dried oregano
- ½ tsp salt
- Low-calorie spray oil
- Salt & pepper to taste

NUTRITION

- Calories: 200
- Protein: 30g
- Total Fat: 4g
- Saturated Fat: 1g
- Carbs: 8g
- Fibre: 2g
- Sugars: 5g

METHOD

1 Toss the chicken slices and vegetables in the cayenne pepper, cumin, oregano and salt.

2 Give the seasoned ingredients a light spray of oil and place in the basket of the air fryer.

3 Cook at 180°C (350°F) for 12-14 minutes, shaking the basket or stirring the contents halfway through.

4 Make sure the chicken is cooked through and piping hot. Season and serve.

CHICKEN & ASPARAGUS FIVE SPICE

Serves 4

INGREDIENTS

- 500g skinless chicken breast, sliced
- 2 tsp Chinese Five Spice powder
- 2 red onions, sliced
- 200g asparagus tips
- Low-calorie spray oil
- Salt & pepper to taste

NUTRITION

- Calories: 180
- Protein: 30g
- Total Fat: 3g
- Saturated Fat: 1g
- Carbs: 6g
- Fibre: 2g
- Sugars: 3g

METHOD

1 Toss the chicken slices and vegetables in the 5 spice powder.

2 Give the seasoned chicken, onions, asparagus a light spray of oil and place in the basket of the air fryer.

3 Cook at 180°C (350°F) for 12-14 minutes, shaking the basket or stirring the contents halfway through.

4 Make sure the chicken is cooked through and piping hot. Season and serve.

GINGER FIRE WINGS

Serves 4

INGREDIENTS

- 3 red chillies, deseeded & sliced
- 1 green pepper, deseeded & sliced
- 1 tbsp freshly grated ginger
- 3 garlic cloves, peeled
- 1 tsp salt
- 1 tsp brown sugar
- 16 chicken wings
- Low-calorie spray oil
- Salt & pepper to taste

NUTRITION

- Calories: 420
- Protein: 28g
- Total Fat: 30g
- Saturated Fat: 8g
- Carbs: 6g
- Fibre: 1g
- Sugars: 3g

METHOD

1 Use a pestle and mortar to grind together the chillies, pepper, ginger, garlic, salt & sugar until blended into a paste.

2 Smother the paste over the chicken wings (if possible leave to marinate for an hour or two).

3 Spray each wing with oil and place in the air fryer basket.

4 Cook for 25 minutes on 200°C (400°F) or until the wings are cooked through and piping hot.

SWEET SOY DRUMMERS

Serves 4

INGREDIENTS

- 60ml soy sauce
- 2 tbsp honey
- 2 garlic cloves, crushed
- 12 chicken drumsticks
- Low-calorie spray oil
- Salt & pepper to taste

NUTRITION

- Calories: 380
- Protein: 28g
- Total Fat: 22g
- Saturated Fat: 6g
- Carbs: 12g
- Fibre: 0g
- Sugars: 10g

METHOD

1 Combine together the soy sauce, honey & garlic.

2 Smother the sticky soy over the chicken drumsticks (if possible leave to marinate for an hour or two).

3 Spray each drumstick with oil and place in the air fryer basket.

4 Cook for 25 minutes on 200°C (400°F) or until the chicken is cooked through and piping hot.

SIMPLY CRISPY WINGS

Serves 4

INGREDIENTS

- 16 chicken wings
- 2-3 tsp baking powder
- 1 tsp garlic powder
- 1 tsp salt
- Low-calorie spray oil
- Lemon wedges to serve
- Salt & pepper to taste

NUTRITION

- Calories: 380
- Protein: 28g
- Total Fat: 28g
- Saturated Fat: 8g
- Carbs: 1g
- Fibre: 0g
- Sugars: 0g

METHOD

1 Toss the chicken wings with baking powder, garlic and salt.

2 Leave to sit in the fridge for a few hours.

3 Spray each wing with oil and place in the air fryer basket.

4 Cook for 25 minutes on 200°C (400°F) or until cooked through and piping hot.

CHICKEN & OLIVES

Serves 4

INGREDIENTS

- 4 large chicken breasts
- 2 courgettes, sliced
- 150g cherry tomatoes, halved
- 75g pitted black olives, halved
- 1 tsp garlic powder
- 1 tsp dried basil
- 1 tsp dried oregano
- 1 lemon zest & juice
- 2 tbsp olive oil
- Salt & pepper to taste
- 2 tbsp freshly chopped parsley

NUTRITION

- Calories: 430
- Protein: 52g
- Total Fat: 15g
- Saturated Fat: 2.5g
- Carbs: 10g
- Fibre: 3g
- Sugars: 5g

METHOD

1 In a large bowl, combine the courgette slices, cherry tomatoes and olives with 1 tbsp of olive oil, garlic powder, salt and pepper. Toss to coat evenly. Add the seasoned vegetables to the air fryer basket and cook at 180°C (350°F) for 8 minutes.

2 While the vegetables are cooking, season the chicken breasts with the dried basil, oregano, lemon zest and the remaining olive oil. After the vegetables have cooked for 8 minutes, add the seasoned chicken breasts to the air fryer basket on top of the vegetables.

3 Continue cooking for an additional 16-20 minutes or until the chicken is cooked through and piping hot. Once done, drizzle with lemon juice and sprinkle with chopped parsley. Season and serve.

MEAT

HONEY GLAZED GAMMON

Serves 4

INGREDIENTS

- 2 tbsp honey
- 2 tbsp Dijon mustard
- 1 tsp apple cider vinegar
- 1 tsp garlic powder
- 1 tsp dried thyme
- 4 lean gammon steaks (about 200g each)
- 200g fresh spinach leaves
- 1 red pepper, sliced
- 1 red onion, sliced
- Low-calorie spray oil
- Salt & pepper to taste

NUTRITION

- Calories: 350
- Protein: 40g
- Total Fat: 9g
- Saturated Fat: 3g
- Carbs: 25g
- Fibre: 4g
- Sugars: 16g

METHOD

1 In a small bowl, whisk together the honey, Dijon mustard, apple cider vinegar, garlic powder and dried thyme until well combined. Season with a pinch of salt and pepper to taste.

2 Place the sliced red onion, pepper and spinach leaves in the air fryer basket. Lightly spray with low-calorie spray oil and season. Cook at 180°C (350°F) for 5 minutes until the vegetables start to soften.

3 After 5 minutes, push the vegetables to the sides of the air fryer basket and place the gammon steaks in the centre. Lightly spray the gammon steaks with oil and brush the tops with the honey mustard glaze. Cook for 5 minutes.

4 Flip the gammon steaks, brush the other side with the glaze, and continue cooking for another 5-7 minutes, or until the gammon is heated through and the glaze is caramelized and slightly sticky.

5 Check the seasoning and serve.

PORK BURGERS

Serves 4

INGREDIENTS

- 500g lean pork mince (5% fat or less)
- 1 small apple, grated
- 1 small onion, finely chopped
- 1 tsp dried sage
- 1 tsp Dijon mustard
- 4 whole-grain buns
- ½ head lettuce, shredded
- Salt & pepper to taste
- Low-calorie spray oil

NUTRITION

- Calories: 380
- Protein: 28g
- Total Fat: 12g
- Saturated Fat: 4g
- Carbs: 40g
- Fibre: 5g
- Sugars: 6g

METHOD

1 In a large bowl, combine the mince, grated apple, onion, Dijon mustard, salt, and pepper.

2 Mix until all ingredients are well combined. Divide into 4 equal portions and shape each portion into a patty, about 1.5cm thick.

3 Place the patties in the air fryer basket and spray with low-calorie oil. Cook for 10-12 minutes, flipping halfway through, until the burgers are cooked through.

4 Allow the burgers to rest for a couple of minutes and serve on whole-grain buns with shredded lettuce and the toppings of your choice.

PORK CHOPS & BABY POTATOES

Serves 4

INGREDIENTS

- 4 lean bone-in pork chops
- 1 tsp garlic powder
- 2 tsp dried rosemary
- 1 tsp paprika
- 1 tsp ground cumin
- 1 red onion, sliced
- 2 red bell peppers, sliced
- 200g baby potatoes, halved
- Low-calorie spray oil
- Salt & pepper to taste

NUTRITION

- Calories: 400
- Protein: 38g
- Total Fat: 12g
- Saturated Fat: 3.5g
- Carbs: 30g
- Fibre: 5g
- Sugars: 5g

METHOD

1 Lightly spray an air fryer-safe dish with low-calorie spray oil. Add the sliced red onion, peppers and potatoes. Season with garlic powder, salt, pepper, and half of the rosemary. Toss to coat the vegetables evenly.

2 In a separate bowl, rub the pork chops with the paprika, cumin, the remaining rosemary, and a bit of salt and pepper.

3 Put the vegetables in the air fryer and cook at 180°C (350°F) for 10 minutes to start softening them. After 10 minutes, add the seasoned pork chops on top of the vegetables. Continue cooking for an additional 12-15 minutes, flipping the pork chops halfway through to ensure even cooking.

4 Let the pork chops rest for a few minutes, season and serve.

SPICED LAMB STIR-FRY

Serves 4

INGREDIENTS

- 500g lean lamb leg steaks, sliced into thin strips
- 2 red onions, sliced
- 2 peppers, sliced
- 2 courgettes, sliced
- 1 tsp each garlic powder, cumin & coriander
- ½ tsp each paprika & cinnamon
- 1 tbsp lemon juice
- 2 tbsp freshly chopped mint
- Low-calorie spray oil
- Salt & pepper to taste

NUTRITION

- Calories: 320
- Protein: 35g
- Total Fat: 14g
- Saturated Fat: 5g
- Carbs: 14g
- Fibre: 5g
- Sugars: 8g

METHOD

1 Spray an air fryer-safe dish with low-calorie spray oil. Add the sliced red onions, peppers, courgette and garlic. Cook in the air fryer at 180°C (350°F) for 5 minutes until the vegetables start to soften.

2 In a large bowl, combine the lamb strips with cumin, coriander, paprika, cinnamon, lemon juice, salt and pepper.

3 Add the lamb to the air fryer with the vegetables. Cook at 180°C (350°F) for 10-12 minutes, stirring halfway through, until the lamb is cooked to your liking and the vegetables are tender.

4 Season, sprinkle with chopped mint and serve.

THAI PORK

Serves 6

INGREDIENTS

- 2 onions, sliced
- 2 garlic cloves, crushed
- 1 red pepper, sliced
- 2 carrots, cut into thin batons
- 500g pork tenderloin, cut into strips
- 2 tbsp Thai red curry paste
- 1 tbsp water
- 100ml low-fat coconut milk
- 300g/9oz pre-cooked or 'straight to wok' noodles
- 2 tbsp freshly chopped coriander
- 2 tbsp chopped peanuts
- Low-calorie spray oil
- Salt & pepper to taste

NUTRITION

- Calories: 420
- Protein: 35g
- Total Fat: 14g
- Saturated Fat: 7g
- Carbs: 40g
- Fibre: 6g
- Sugars: 10g

METHOD

1 Lightly spray an air fryer-safe dish with low-calorie spray oil. Add the sliced onions, garlic, red pepper, and carrot batons. Cook in the air fryer at 180°C (350°F) for 5 minutes.

2 Add the pork strips to the dish along with the Thai red curry paste and 1 tbsp of water. Combine pork evenly with the curry paste. Cook for 10 minutes, stirring halfway through to ensure the pork is evenly cooked.

3 Pour in the coconut milk and stir in the pre-cooked noodles, making sure everything is well combined. Cook for an additional 2-4 minutes, or until the noodles are heated through and the dish is piping hot.

4 Season to taste. Garnish with freshly chopped coriander and chopped peanuts.

PORK TENDERLOIN & APPLE

Serves 4

INGREDIENTS

- 2 onions, sliced
- 2 garlic cloves, crushed
- 2 carrots, cut into thin batons
- 200g mushrooms, sliced
- 500g pork tenderloin, cut into strips
- 60ml pure apple juice
- 1 tsp Dijon mustard
- 1 bunch spring onions, sliced length-ways
- 1 apple, thinly sliced for garnish
- Low-calorie spray oil
- 1 tsp dried thyme or rosemary
- Salt & pepper to taste

NUTRITION

- Calories: 330
- Protein: 38g
- Total Fat: 10g
- Saturated Fat: 3g
- Carbs: 22g
- Fibre: 4g
- Sugars: 14g

METHOD

1 Lightly spray an air fryer-safe dish with low-calorie spray oil. Add the sliced onions, crushed garlic, carrot batons, and sliced mushrooms to the dish. Cook in the air fryer at 180°C (350°F) for 5 minutes until the vegetables start to soften.

2 Add the pork tenderloin strips to the dish. In a small bowl, mix the pure apple juice with Dijon mustard and dried thyme or rosemary. Pour the mixture over the pork and vegetables. Cook in the air fryer for 12-14 minutes, stirring halfway through.

3 Once cooked, remove the dish from the air fryer and season. Garnish with the sliced spring onions and thin apple slices to serve.

BEEF, BEANS & RICE

Serves 4

INGREDIENTS

- 1 onion, sliced
- 2 garlic cloves, crushed
- 120ml tomato passata
- 1 tin (400g) mixed beans, drained & rinsed
- 1 tbsp tomato puree
- 1 tsp dried rosemary
- ½ beef stock cube
- ½ tsp each brown sugar, paprika & ground cumin
- 300g pre-cooked brown rice
- 1 handful fresh spinach
- 1 tbsp fat-free Greek yoghurt
- 2 tbsp freshly chopped flat-leaf parsley
- Low-calorie spray oil
- Salt & pepper to taste

NUTRITION

- Calories: 450
- Protein: 35g
- Total Fat: 12g
- Saturated Fat: 4.5g
- Carbs: 50g
- Fibre: 8g
- Sugars: 6g

METHOD

1 Lightly spray an air fryer-safe dish with low-calorie spray oil. Add the mince and onions. Cook in the air fryer at 180°C (350°F) for 10 minutes, stirring halfway through.

2 Stir in the garlic, paprika, cumin, tomato passata, puree, dried rosemary, crumbled beef stock cube, and sugar. Mix well and cook for another 5 minutes at 180°C (350°F).

3 Add the mixed beans and a handful of fresh spinach to the dish. Cook for an additional 5 minutes, stirring halfway through, until the beans are heated through, the spinach is wilted, and everything is well mixed with the beef and sauce.

4 Stir in the pre-cooked brown rice, making sure it is evenly coated with the sauce. Cook for 3-5 minutes at 180°C (350°F), or until the rice is heated through.

5 Remove the dish from the air fryer. Stir in the fat-free Greek yoghurt, season and garnish with parsley before serving.

SAUSAGE GNOCCHI

Serves 4

INGREDIENTS

- 8 lean pork sausages
- 3 peppers, sliced
- 1 onion, sliced
- ½ tsp garlic powder
- 1 tsp dried basil or oregano
- 800g gnocchi
- Low-calorie spray oil
- Salt & pepper to taste

NUTRITION

- Calories: 500
- Protein: 28g
- Total Fat: 18g
- Saturated Fat: 6g
- Carbs: 60g
- Fibre: 7g
- Sugars: 6g

METHOD

1 Place the sliced peppers, onion, garlic powder, and dried basil or oregano in the air fryer. Lightly spray with low-calorie oil and cook for 10 minutes.

2 Remove the vegetables from the air fryer and set aside. Add the sausages and gnocchi to the air fryer. Spray with low-calorie oil and cook for 20 minutes, or until the sausages are cooked through and the gnocchi starts to crisp up.

3 After this time remove the sausages and slice them into 1cm thick discs. Add the sliced sausages, sautéed peppers, and onions back into the air fryer with the gnocchi.

4 Cook for an additional 5 minutes, or until the gnocchi is crispy on the outside and tender on the inside. Season and serve hot.

GARLIC BEEF & BEANSPROUTS

Serves 4

INGREDIENTS

- 2 onions, sliced
- 8 garlic cloves, finely sliced
- 1 tbsp freshly grated ginger
- 2 tsp olive oil or vegetable oil
- 400g lean steak, sliced
- 200g fresh beansprouts
- Low-calorie spray oil
- 1 tsp sesame oil
- Salt & pepper to taste

NUTRITION

- Calories: 350
- Protein: 32g
- Total Fat: 14g
- Saturated Fat: 4.5g
- Carbs: 20g
- Fibre: 4g
- Sugars: 5g

METHOD

1 Place the sliced onions and grated ginger in the air fryer and spray with low-calorie oil. Cook for 3 minutes at 180°C (350°F) to allow the onions to soften and the ginger to release its aroma.

2 After 3 minutes, add the finely sliced garlic to the onion and ginger mixture. Continue cooking for another 2 minutes, ensuring the garlic cooks but does not burn.

3 Add the sliced steak to the air fryer and cook for 4 minutes until the steak is browned. Toss in the fresh beansprouts and cook for an additional 2-3 minutes, or until the beansprouts are slightly softened and everything is cooked through.

4 Drizzle with sesame oil, season and serve.

CHEESE-STUFFED MEATBALLS

Serves 4

INGREDIENTS

- 600g lean beef mince
- 1 tsp garlic powder
- 1 tsp dried oregano
- 2 tbsp fresh breadcrumbs
- 150g low-fat cheddar cheese, cut into 1cm cubes
- 400g tomato passata
- ½ tsp brown sugar
- ½ tsp salt
- 2 tbsp tomato puree
- Low-calorie spray oil
- Salt & pepper to taste

NUTRITION

- Calories: 430
- Protein: 35g
- Total Fat: 18g
- Saturated Fat: 8g
- Carbs: 28g
- Fibre: 5g
- Sugars: 7g

METHOD

1 In a food processor, combine the beef mince, garlic powder, dried oregano, and breadcrumbs. Pulse a few times until the mixture is well combined.

2 Take the mixture and form 12-16 small meatballs with your hands. Push a cube of cheese into the centre of each meatball, ensuring the cheese is completely covered by the meat.

3 Lightly spray an air fryer-safe dish with low-calorie spray oil. Place the meatballs in the dish, ensuring they are evenly spaced. Cook in the air fryer at 180°C (350°F) for 15 minutes, shaking the dish halfway through to ensure even cooking.

4 After 15 minutes, remove the dish and pour in the tomato passata. Stir in the salt, brown sugar, and tomato puree. Return the dish to the air fryer and cook for an additional 5-10 minutes, until the meatballs are cooked through. Season and serve.

LAMB 'KEBAB' PITTAS

Serves 4

INGREDIENTS

- 1 tbsp dried oregano
- 1 tbsp olive oil
- 3 garlic cloves, crushed
- 3 tbsp red wine
- Zest and juice of 1 lemon
- 600g lean lamb fillet, cut into 2cm cubes
- 4 large brown pita breads
- 4 tbsp fat-free Greek yoghurt
- 1 baby gem lettuce, shredded
- Lemon wedges, to serve
- Salt & pepper to taste

NUTRITION

- Calories: 490
- Protein: 36g
- Total Fat: 18g
- Saturated Fat: 6g
- Carbs: 42g
- Fibre: 5g
- Sugars: 3g

METHOD

1 In a large bowl, combine the oregano, olive oil, crushed garlic, red wine, lemon zest, and lemon juice. Add the cubed lamb, tossing to coat the meat evenly. Cover and refrigerate, allowing it to marinate for as long as possible, ideally overnight.

2 Remove the marinated lamb from the bowl and place it in the air fryer. Cook at 180°C (350°F) for 20-25 minutes, or until the lamb is cooked to your liking, stirring halfway through to ensure even cooking.

3 Warm the pitta breads, then fill each with the cooked lamb, shredded lettuce, and a dollop of fat-free Greek yoghurt. Serve with lemon wedges on the side.

MOROCCAN LAMB

Serves 4

INGREDIENTS

- 1 onion, sliced
- 2 tsp freshly grated ginger
- 2 garlic cloves, crushed
- 50g black olives, halved
- 400g lamb neck fillet, cut into strips
- 2 tsp cornflour
- 60ml lamb stock
- ½ tsp each ground nutmeg & cinnamon
- 50g sultanas
- 250g pre-cooked couscous
- 2 tbsp freshly chopped coriander
- Low-calorie spray oil
- Salt & pepper to taste

NUTRITION

- Calories: 450
- Protein: 28g
- Total Fat: 18g
- Saturated Fat: 7g
- Carbs: 45g
- Fibre: 5g
- Sugars: 10g

METHOD

1 In a large bowl, combine the sliced onion, freshly grated ginger, and crushed garlic. Lightly spray with low-calorie spray oil and toss to coat evenly. Transfer to an air fryer-safe dish and cook at 180°C (350°F) for 5 minutes.

2 Season the lamb with salt, pepper, ground nutmeg, and cinnamon. Toss the lamb with the cornflour to lightly coat and add the seasoned lamb to the dish with the onions. Stir in the lamb stock and cook for another 7-10 minutes at 180°C (350°F).

3 Stir in the olives, pre-cooked couscous and sultanas. Cook for an additional 5-7 minutes or until the lamb is cooked and everything is piping hot.

4 Adjust the seasoning and serve with freshly chopped coriander sprinkled over.

STEAK & BROCCOLI STIR-FRY

Serves 4

INGREDIENTS

- 1 onion, sliced
- 1 red chilli, sliced
- 3 garlic cloves, crushed
- 250g purple sprouting broccoli, roughly chopped
- 400g lean steak, sliced
- 250g pre-cooked brown rice
- 2 tbsp soy sauce
- Low-calorie spray oil
- Salt & pepper to taste

NUTRITION

- Calories: 330
- Protein: 28g
- Total Fat: 9g
- Saturated Fat: 3g
- Carbs: 35g
- Fibre: 5g
- Sugars: 2g

METHOD

1 In a large bowl, combine the sliced onion, sliced red chili, crushed garlic, and chopped broccoli. Lightly spray with low-cal spray oil and toss to coat evenly. Transfer to an air fryer-safe dish and cook at 180°C (350°F) for 5-7 minutes.

2 Season the sliced steak and add to the vegetables along with the pre-cooked rice and soy sauce to the dish with the vegetables. Toss everything together to combine and ensure the ingredients are well-coated.

3 Continue cooking at 180°C (350°F) for an additional 7-10 minutes, stirring occasionally, until the steak is cooked to your liking and the broccoli is tender.

4 Adjust the seasoning and serve.

COCOA BEEF

Serves 4

INGREDIENTS

- 400g lean steak, sliced
- 1 tbsp cocoa powder
- 2 tbsp tomato puree/paste
- 3 tbsp water
- 1 onion, sliced
- 1 red chilli, finely sliced
- 2 carrots, cut into thin batons
- 2 red peppers, sliced
- 2 garlic cloves, crushed
- 1 bunch spring onions, sliced length-ways
- Low-calorie spray oil
- Salt & pepper to taste

NUTRITION

- Calories: 310
- Protein: 26g
- Total Fat: 10g
- Saturated Fat: 3g
- Carbs: 25g
- Fibre: 6g
- Sugars: 10g

METHOD

1 Combine the sliced steak with cocoa powder, tomato puree, water, salt, and pepper. Marinate in the fridge for 15-30 minutes.

2 Toss sliced onion, chili, carrots, red peppers, and garlic in low-calorie spray oil. Cook in an air fryer-safe dish at 180°C (350°F) for 8-10 minutes until softened.

3 Add marinated steak and any remaining marinade to the dish. If needed, add another splash of water. Stir to combine.

4 Cook for another 7-10 minutes at 180°C (350°F), stirring occasionally until steak is cooked and vegetables are tender. Stir in sliced spring onions, adjust seasoning, and serve.

BEEF KEEMA

Serves 4

INGREDIENTS

- 2 onions, finely chopped
- 2 garlic cloves, crushed
- 800g lean beef mince
- 1 small tin (200g) tinned chopped tomatoes
- 2 tbsp tomato puree/paste
- 1 tbsp medium curry powder
- ½ beef stock cube
- ½ tsp brown sugar & salt
- 200g frozen peas
- 2 tbsp freshly chopped coriander
- Low-calorie spray oil
- Salt & pepper to taste

NUTRITION

- Calories: 350
- Protein: 35g
- Total Fat: 15g
- Saturated Fat: 6g
- Carbs: 20g
- Fibre: 5g
- Sugars: 6g

METHOD

1 In a large bowl, combine the finely chopped onion and crushed garlic. Lightly spray with low-calorie oil. Transfer the mixture to an air fryer-safe dish and cook at 180°C (350°F) for 5 minutes until the onion is softened and aromatic.

2 Add the beef mince, ensuring it's broken up. Return the dish to the air fryer and cook at 180°C (350°F) for 8-10 minutes, stirring occasionally, until the beef is browned and cooked through.

3 After 10 minutes stir in the curry powder, chopped tomatoes, tomato puree, crumbled beef stock cube, brown sugar, salt and peas.

4 Return the dish to the air fryer and continue cooking at 180°C (350°F) for an additional 5-7 minutes, or until the peas are heated through and the sauce has thickened. Stir in the freshly chopped coriander adjust the seasoning and serve.

BEEF & CHICKPEA STEW

Serves 4

INGREDIENTS

- 1 onion, finely chopped
- 2 garlic cloves, crushed
- 2 carrots, finely chopped
- 400g lean beef mince
- 1 tin (400g) chickpeas, drained and rinsed
- 1 tin (400g) chopped tomatoes
- 1 tbsp tomato puree
- 1 tsp each ground cumin & cinnamon
- ½ tsp ground turmeric
- 1 tbsp honey
- 1 tbsp lemon juice
- 2 tbsp freshly chopped coriander
- Low-calorie spray oil
- Salt & pepper to taste

NUTRITION

- Calories: 410
- Protein: 35g
- Total Fat: 15g
- Saturated Fat: 6g
- Carbs: 37g
- Fibre: 9g
- Sugars: 12g

METHOD

1 In a large bowl, combine the finely chopped onion, crushed garlic, and chopped carrots. Lightly spray with low-calorie oil and toss to coat. Transfer the mixture to an air fryer-safe dish and cook at 180°C (350°F) for 8-10 minutes, stirring halfway through.

2 After this time add the beef mince to the dish. Break up the meat and combine with the vegetables. Cook for 8-10 minutes, stirring occasionally, until the beef is browned and cooked through. Once the beef is cooked, stir in the ground cumin, cinnamon, and turmeric. Cook for another 2 minutes to allow the spices to release their aromas.

3 Add the tinned chopped tomatoes, drained chickpeas, tomato puree, honey, and lemon juice to the dish. Stir to combine. Return the dish to the air fryer and cook for an additional 10-12 minutes at 180°C (350°F), stirring occasionally, until the sauce has thickened and everything is piping hot.

4 Adjust the seasoning, sprinkle with freshly chopped coriander and serve.

RICH RAGU

Serves 4

INGREDIENTS

- 1 onion, finely chopped
- 2 garlic cloves, crushed
- 2 carrots, finely chopped
- 400g lean beef mince
- 1 tin (400g) chopped tomatoes
- 1 tbsp sundried tomato puree
- 1 tsp dried thyme
- ½ beef stock cube
- ½ tsp brown sugar
- 1 tbsp Worcestershire sauce
- Low-calorie spray oil
- Salt & pepper to taste

NUTRITION

- Calories: 320
- Protein: 31g
- Total Fat: 12g
- Saturated Fat: 5g
- Carbs: 21g
- Fibre: 5g
- Sugars: 9g

METHOD

1 In a large bowl, combine the finely chopped onion, crushed garlic and chopped carrots. Lightly spray with low-calorie oil and toss to coat. Transfer the mixture to an air fryer-safe dish and cook at 180°C (350°F) for 8-10 minutes, stirring halfway through.

2 After the vegetables are softened, add the beef mince to the dish. Break it up to combine with the vegetables. Cook for 8-10 minutes, stirring occasionally, until the beef is browned and cooked through.

3 Add the tinned chopped tomatoes, sundried tomato puree, dried thyme, beef stock cube, brown sugar, and Worcestershire sauce to the dish. Stir to combine.

4 Return the dish to the air fryer and cook for an additional 10-12 minutes at 180°C (350°F), stirring occasionally, until the sauce has thickened. Adjust the seasoning and serve.

STEAK & WHITE BEAN BAKE

Serves 4

INGREDIENTS

- 1 onion, sliced
- 2 garlic cloves, crushed
- 400g lean steak, sliced
- 200g cherry tomatoes
- 400g tinned cannellini beans, drained
- 1 tbsp tomato puree
- 1 tsp dried basil
- ½ tsp brown sugar
- 2 tbsp freshly chopped flat leaf parsley
- Low-calorie spray oil
- Salt & pepper to taste

NUTRITION

- Calories: 340
- Protein: 31g
- Total Fat: 10g
- Saturated Fat: 3g
- Carbs: 27g
- Fibre: 8g
- Sugars: 6g

METHOD

1 In a large bowl, combine the sliced onions and garlic. Lightly spray with oil and toss to coat. Place the mixture in an air fryer-safe dish and cook at 180°C (350°F) for 5 minutes until the onions are softened.

2 While the onions and garlic are cooking, toss the sliced steak with the tomato puree, dried herbs, and brown sugar in a separate bowl. After the onions are ready, add the steak, cherry tomatoes, and drained cannellini beans to the air fryer-safe dish. Stir to combine everything evenly.

3 Return the dish to the air fryer and cook for an additional 8-12 minutes at 180°C (350°F), stirring halfway through. Check the steak is cooked to your liking. Season, sprinkle with freshly chopped parsley and serve.

SPANISH FRIED RICE

Serves 4

INGREDIENTS

- 2 red onions, chopped
- 1 tsp garlic powder
- 1 carrot, finely chopped
- 1 pepper, finely chopped
- 125g frozen peas
- 120g chorizo, finely diced
- 1 tsp paprika
- 1 tsp salt
- 500g pre-cooked rice
- 2 eggs, beaten
- 2 tbsp freshly chopped flat leaf parsley
- Low-calorie spray oil
- Salt & pepper to taste

NUTRITION

- Calories: 410
- Protein: 16g
- Total Fat: 17g
- Saturated Fat: 6g
- Carbs: 46g
- Fibre: 6g
- Sugars: 5g

METHOD

1 In a large bowl, combine the chopped red onions, garlic, chopped carrot, red pepper, peas, and finely diced chorizo. Spray with low-calorie oil, season and and toss to coat.

2 Place the mixture in an air fryer-safe dish and cook at 180°C (350°F) for 8-10 minutes, stirring halfway through.

3 After this time add the paprika, salt, and pre-cooked rice to the dish. Pour the beaten eggs and cook for an additional 8-12 minutes at 180°C (350°F), stirring occasionally, until everything is cooked through.

4 Once the dish is cooked, remove it from the air fryer. Season, sprinkle with freshly chopped parsley and serve.

CHINESE PORK & CABBAGE

Serves 4

INGREDIENTS

- 1 onion, sliced
- 1 tsp garlic powder
- 2 carrots, cut into thin batons
- 125g shitake mushrooms, sliced
- 500g pork tenderloin, sliced into strips
- 2 Pak Choi, roughly chopped
- 1 tbsp soy sauce
- 2 tsp rice wine vinegar
- 6 spring onions, sliced lengthways
- Low-calorie spray oil
- Salt & pepper to taste

NUTRITION

- Calories: 280
- Protein: 29g
- Total Fat: 10g
- Saturated Fat: 2g
- Carbs: 16g
- Fibre: 4g
- Sugars: 6g

METHOD

1 Put the onions, garlic, carrots and mushrooms in a bowl. Spray with oil, season and combine. Add to the air fryer basket and cook at 180°C (350°F) for 10 minutes.

2 After this time add the pork, Pak Choi, soy sauce & rice wine vinegar, spray with oil combine well and cook for another 12-14 minutes or until the pork is cooked through and piping hot.

3 Season and serve with the spring onion ribbons.

BALSAMIC BEEF & POTATOES

Serves 4

INGREDIENTS

- 500g beef sirloin, sliced into strips
- 300g baby potatoes, halved
- 2 courgettes, sliced
- 1 red pepper, sliced
- 150g cherry tomatoes, halved
- 1 red onion, sliced into wedges
- 1 tsp garlic powder
- 2 tbsp balsamic vinegar
- 2 tbsp olive oil
- 1 tsp dried oregano
- 1 tsp dried basil
- Salt & pepper to taste
- 2 tbsp freshly chopped basil

NUTRITION

- Calories: 420
- Protein: 30g
- Total Fat: 18g
- Saturated Fat: 4g
- Carbs: 35g
- Fibre: 5g
- Sugars: 6g

METHOD

1 In a large bowl, toss the halved baby potatoes with 1 tbsp of olive oil, salt, pepper, oregano and dried basil. Place the seasoned potatoes in the air fryer basket and cook at 180°C (350°F) for 10 minutes.

2 While the potatoes are cooking, combine the courgette slices, pepper, tomatoes and red onion in the same bowl. Add the remaining olive oil, garlic powder and a bit more salt and pepper. Toss to coat.

3 After the potatoes have cooked for 10 minutes, add the mixed vegetables to the air fryer basket. Continue cooking at 180°C (350°F) for another 8 minutes. Meanwhile, season the beef strips with balsamic vinegar, salt and pepper. After the vegetables and potatoes have cooked, add the seasoned beef strips to the air fryer basket on top of the vegetables and potatoes.

4 Cook for an additional 8-12 minutes, stirring once halfway through, until the beef is cooked to your liking, the vegetables are tender and the potatoes are golden. Sprinkle with freshly chopped basil and serve.

FISH & SEAFOOD

SESAME TUNA STEAKS

Serves 4

INGREDIENTS

- 4 tuna steaks (about 150g each)
- 300g broccoli florets
- 2 tbsp soy sauce
- 1 tbsp honey
- 1 tbsp rice vinegar
- 1 tbsp sesame oil (divided)
- ½ tsp garlic powder
- 1 tsp fresh ginger, grated
- 1 tbsp sesame seeds, toasted
- Low-calorie spray oil
- Salt & pepper, to taste

NUTRITION

- Calories: 350 kcal
- Protein: 35g
- Total Fat: 15g
- Saturated Fat: 3g
- Carbohydrates: 15g
- Fibre: 4g
- Sugars: 7g

METHOD

1 In a small bowl combine the soy sauce, honey, rice vinegar, ½ tbsp sesame oil, garlic powder and grated ginger to create a marinade.

2 Place the tuna steaks in a shallow dish and pour the marinade over. Leave for 15-20 minutes.

3 While the tuna is marinating, spray the broccoli florets with oil and season with salt and pepper. In an air fryer-safe dish or directly in the basket, cook the broccoli at 200°C for 5 minutes.

4 After the broccoli has cooked for 5 minutes, push it to one side of the dish or basket. Add the marinated tuna steaks to and cook at 180°C for 4-6 minutes, depending on your preference.

5 Once cooked to your liking drizzle the remaining ½ tbsp of sesame oil over the broccoli. Garnish the tuna steaks with sesame seeds and serve.

HADDOCK WITH SWEET POTATO WEDGES

Serves 4

INGREDIENTS

- 4 haddock fillets (about 150g each)
- 2 large sweet potatoes, cut into wedges
- 50g panko breadcrumbs
- 1 tbsp dried mixed herbs
- 1 tsp garlic powder
- 2 tbsp olive oil
- 1 lemon, zested and juiced
- Low-calorie spray oil
- Salt & pepper, to taste
- 2 tbsp fresh flat leaf parsley, chopped

NUTRITION

- Calories: 420 kcal
- Protein: 35g
- Total Fat: 15g
- Saturated Fat: 3g
- Carbohydrates: 40g
- Fibre: 7g
- Sugars: 8g

METHOD

1 Lightly spray the sweet potato wedges with oil. Season with salt, pepper, and the garlic powder. Place the wedges in an air fryer-safe dish or directly in the air fryer basket. Cook at 200°C for 15 minutes, shaking the basket halfway through, until the wedges are crispy and golden brown.

2 In a small bowl, mix together the panko breadcrumbs, dried mixed herbs, garlic powder, lemon zest, salt, and pepper. Drizzle in 1 tablespoon of olive oil and mix until the breadcrumbs are evenly coated.

3 Place the haddock fillets on a plate and drizzle with the remaining olive oil and lemon juice. Press the herb crumb mixture onto the top of each fillet, ensuring it sticks well.

4 Once the sweet potato wedges have cooked for 15 minutes, move them to one side of the air fryer basket or dish. Place the herb-crusted haddock fillets on the other side. Cook at 180°C for an additional 10-12 minutes, or until the haddock is cooked through and the crust is golden and crispy.

5 Garnish the haddock with parsley and serve with lemon wedges on the side.

COCONUT PRAWNS WITH MANGO SALSA

Serves 4

INGREDIENTS

- 400g large prawns, peeled
- 100g unsweetened desiccated coconut
- 50g panko breadcrumbs
- 2 medium eggs, beaten
- 50g plain flour
- ½ tsp garlic powder
- ½ tsp paprika
- 1 ripe mango, diced
- ½ red pepper, diced
- ¼ red onion, finely chopped
- 1 tbsp fresh coriander, chopped
- Juice of 1 lime
- Low-calorie spray oil
- Salt & pepper, to taste

NUTRITION

- Calories: 350 kcal
- Protein: 25g
- Total Fat: 15g
- Saturated Fat: 8g
- Carbohydrates: 30g
- Fibre: 4g
- Sugars: 10g

METHOD

1 Set up three bowls: one with flour seasoned with garlic powder, paprika, salt, and pepper; one with beaten eggs; and one with the desiccated coconut mixed with panko breadcrumbs.

2 Dredge each prawn in the flour, dip in the egg, then coat with the coconut-panko mixture. Place the prawns in a single layer in the air fryer basket and lightly spray with low-calorie spray oil. Cook at 200°C for 8-10 minutes, flipping halfway through, until golden and crispy.

3 While the prawns are cooking, prepare the mango salsa by mixing the diced mango, red pepper, red onion, coriander, lime juice, and salt in a bowl.

4 Serve the crispy coconut prawns with the mango salsa on the side.

FISH & GREEN BEANS

Serves 4

INGREDIENTS

- 4 boneless white fish fillets (about 150g each)
- 300g baby potatoes, halved
- 200g green beans, trimmed
- 1 tsp garlic powder
- 1 tsp dried rosemary
- 1 tsp dried thyme
- 1 lemon, sliced into rounds
- 2 tbsp olive oil
- 2 tbsp fresh flat leaf parsley, chopped
- Low-calorie spray oil
- Salt & pepper, to taste

NUTRITION

- Calories: 380
- Protein: 32g
- Total Fat: 16g
- Saturated Fat: 3g
- Carbs: 30g
- Fibre: 5g
- Sugars: 2g

METHOD

1 In a small bowl, combine the garlic powder, dried rosemary, dried thyme, olive oil, salt, and pepper. Rub the mixture over the white fish fillets.

2 Lightly spray the baby potatoes with low-calorie spray oil and season with salt and pepper. Place the potatoes in an air fryer-safe dish or directly in the air fryer basket. Cook at 200°C (390°F) for 10 minutes, shaking the basket halfway through.

3 After 10 minutes, add the green beans to the potatoes, lightly spraying with more oil if needed. Lay the white fish fillets on top of the vegetables, and place lemon slices on top of the fish. Cook at 180°C (350°F) for an additional 10-12 minutes, or until the fish is cooked through and flakes easily with a fork, the potatoes are crispy, and the green beans are tender.

4 Garnish with fresh parsley and serve immediately.

SALMON WITH ASPARAGUS

Serves 4

INGREDIENTS

- 4 salmon fillets (about 150g each)
- 300g asparagus
- 1 tsp garlic powder
- 2 tbsp olive oil
- 1 tsp dried oregano
- 1 tsp dried thyme
- 1 lemon, sliced into rounds
- Low-calorie spray oil
- Salt & pepper, to taste
- Fresh parsley, chopped, for garnish

NUTRITION

- Calories: 360
- Protein: 30g
- Total Fat: 22g
- Saturated Fat: 4g
- Carbs: 6g
- Fibre: 3g
- Sugars: 2g

METHOD

1 In a small bowl, combine the garlic powder, olive oil, dried oregano, dried thyme, salt, and pepper. Rub the mixture over the salmon fillets.

2 Lightly spray the asparagus with low-calorie spray oil and season with salt and pepper. Place the asparagus in an air fryer-safe dish or directly in the air fryer basket. 3. 3. Lay the salmon fillets on top of the asparagus, and place lemon slices on top of the salmon. Cook at 180°C (350°F) for 10-12 minutes, or until the salmon is cooked through and flakes easily with a fork, and the asparagus is tender.

3 Garnish with fresh parsley and serve immediately.

SCALLOP RICE-BOWL

Serves 4

INGREDIENTS

- 200g chorizo sausage, diced
- 400g scallops, cleaned
- 300g pre-cooked brown rice
- 1 small onion, finely chopped
- 1 red pepper, diced
- 1 tsp garlic powder
- 1 tsp smoked paprika
- 2 tsp olive oil or sunflower oil
- 2 tbsp fresh parsley, chopped
- Lemon wedges, for serving
- Low-calorie spray oil
- Salt & pepper, to taste

NUTRITION

- Calories: 430
- Protein: 27g
- Total Fat: 20g
- Saturated Fat: 6g
- Carbs: 35g
- Fibre: 4g
- Sugars: 3g

METHOD

1 In an air fryer-safe dish, combine the diced chorizo, onion, and red pepper. Lightly spray with low-calorie spray oil and cook at 180°C (350°F) for 4-5 minutes until the chorizo starts to release its oils and the vegetables soften.

2 Add the scallops, garlic powder, and smoked paprika to the dish. Lightly spray the scallops with low-calorie spray oil. Cook for an additional 6-8 minutes, stirring halfway through, until the scallops are cooked through and slightly browned.

3 Add the rice to the dish and stir to combine. Cook for 3-4 minutes until the rice is heated through

4 Season with salt and pepper. Garnish with chopped parsley and serve with lemon wedges on the side.

CHORIZO & KING PRAWN WRAPS

Serves 4

INGREDIENTS

- 200g chorizo sausage, diced
- 500g king prawns, butterflied
- 2 tsp olive oil
- 1 tsp garlic powder
- 1 red chilli, finely chopped
- 4 soft wholemeal tortilla wraps
- 2 baby gem lettuces, shredded
- 100g low-fat Greek yoghurt
- 1 tbsp lemon juice
- 1 tbsp fresh parsley, chopped
- Lemon wedges, for serving
- Salt & pepper, to taste

NUTRITION

- Calories: 410
- Protein: 30g
- Total Fat: 20g
- Saturated Fat: 6g
- Carbs: 28g
- Fibre: 4g
- Sugars: 4g

METHOD

1 Place the chorizo, garlic powder, chilli and oil in an air fryer-safe dish. Cook at 180°C (350°F) for 4 minutes.

2 Add the butterflied prawns to the dish with the chorizo mixture. Cook for an additional 10-12 minutes or until the prawns are cooked through and piping hot.

3 Meanwhile, in a small bowl, mix the low-fat Greek yoghurt, lemon juice, parsley, salt and pepper.

4 Season the prawn and chorizo mixture. Serve with tortilla wraps, shredded lettuce, and a generous drizzle of the yoghurt sauce. Garnish with lemon wedges.

SUPER SIMPLE SWEET & SOUR

Serves 4

INGREDIENTS

- 400g king prawns, peeled
- 1 red pepper, sliced
- 1 yellow pepper, sliced
- 1 small red onion, sliced
- 100g pineapple chunks (fresh or tinned)
- 2 tbsp rice vinegar or apple cider vinegar
- 1 tbsp honey
- 1 tbsp tomato ketchup
- 1 tsp soy sauce
- 1 tbsp olive oil
- Low-calorie spray oil
- Salt & pepper to taste
- 2 tbsp fresh spring onions, chopped, for garnish

NUTRITION

- Calories: 320
- Protein: 32g
- Total Fat: 10g
- Saturated Fat: 1.5g
- Carbs: 24g
- Fibre: 4g
- Sugars: 14g

METHOD

1 In a small bowl, whisk together the rice vinegar (or apple cider vinegar), honey (or maple syrup), tomato ketchup, and soy sauce to create the homemade sweet and sour sauce.

2 In a large bowl, toss the king prawns with olive oil, salt, and pepper.

3 Add the red pepper, yellow pepper, red onion, and pineapple chunks to an air fryer-safe dish. Spray with low-calorie spray oil and cook in the air fryer at 200°C (390°F) for 5 minutes.

4 Add the seasoned prawns to the dish with the vegetables and pineapple. Drizzle the homemade sweet and sour sauce over the top and stir to combine.

5 Cook for an additional 6-8 minutes, stirring halfway through, until the prawns are cooked through and the sauce is slightly caramelized.

6 Garnish with chopped spring onions and serve immediately.

GARLIC PRAWNS WITH SAUTÉED PEPPERS

Serves 4

INGREDIENTS

- 400g large prawns, peeled
- 1 red pepper, sliced
- 1 yellow pepper, sliced
- 200g fresh spinach leaves
- 1 tsp garlic powder
- 1 tsp smoked paprika
- 1 tbsp olive oil
- Low-calorie spray oil
- Salt & pepper to taste
- Lemon wedges, for serving

NUTRITION

- Calories: 280
- Protein: 32g
- Total Fat: 12g
- Saturated Fat: 2g
- Carbs: 10g
- Fibre: 4g
- Sugars: 5g

METHOD

1 In a large bowl, combine the prawns with garlic powder, smoked paprika, olive oil, salt, and pepper.

2 Lightly spray the sliced red and yellow peppers with oil and place them in the air fryer basket in a single layer and cook the peppers at 200°C (390°F) for 5 minutes.

3 After 5 minutes, add the seasoned prawns and fresh spinach leaves to the basket with the peppers, ensuring everything is spread out evenly.

4 Cook for an additional 8-10 minutes, shaking the basket halfway through, until the prawns are cooked through and the spinach is wilted.

5 Serve with lemon wedges on the side.

THAI PRAWN STIR-FRY

Serves 4

INGREDIENTS

- 400g large prawns, peeled
- 2 tbsp Thai red curry paste
- 1 red pepper, sliced
- 1 courgette, sliced
- 1 red onion, sliced
- 100g bean sprouts
- 100g shredded cabbage
- 100g sugar snap peas
- 1 carrot, julienned
- 200ml low-fat coconut milk
- 1 tbsp olive oil
- 2 tbsp fresh coriander, chopped
- Low-calorie spray oil
- Salt & pepper to taste
- Lime wedges, for serving

NUTRITION

- Calories: 420
- Protein: 32g
- Total Fat: 20g
- Saturated Fat: 10g
- Carbs: 22g
- Fibre: 6g
- Sugars: 8g

METHOD

1 Lightly spray an air fryer-safe dish with low-calorie spray oil. Add the red pepper, courgette, red onion, shredded cabbage, sugar snap peas, and julienned carrot to the dish. Season with a pinch of salt and pepper and cook in the air fryer at 180°C (350°F) for 5 minutes.

2 In a bowl, combine the prawns with the Thai red curry paste and olive oil, ensuring they are evenly coated. Add the seasoned prawns and bean sprouts to the dish with the partially cooked vegetables. Pour the coconut milk over the top, stirring gently to combine.

3 Cook at 180°C (350°F) for 8-10 minutes, stirring halfway through, until the prawns are cooked through, and the vegetables are tender.

4 Garnish with chopped coriander and serve with lime wedges.

SALT & PEPPER PRAWNS WITH VEGGIES

Serves 4

INGREDIENTS

- 400g large prawns, peeled
- 1 red pepper, sliced
- 1 courgette, sliced
- 1 red onion, sliced
- 1 tsp black pepper
- ½ tsp white pepper
- ½ tsp garlic powder
- 1 tbsp olive oil
- Low-calorie spray oil
- 2 tbsp fresh coriander, chopped
- Lemon wedges, for serving
- Salt to taste

NUTRITION

- Calories: 320
- Protein: 34g
- Total Fat: 12g
- Saturated Fat: 2g
- Carbs: 14g
- Fibre: 4g
- Sugars: 6g

METHOD

1 In a large bowl, combine the prawns, black pepper, white pepper, garlic powder, olive oil and salt.

2 Lightly spray the sliced red pepper, courgette, and red onion with oil and season with a pinch of salt and pepper. Place the vegetables in the air fryer basket in a single layer and cook at 200°C (390°F) for 5 minutes.

3 After 5 minutes, add prawns to the air fryer basket with the vegetables, ensuring they are in a single layer. Cook for an additional 8-10 minutes, shaking the basket halfway through, until the prawns are cooked through and slightly crispy, and the vegetables are tender.

4 Garnish with 2 tbsp of chopped coriander and serve with lemon wedges.

CRISPY GARLIC PRAWNS

Serves 4

INGREDIENTS

- 400g large prawns, peeled
- 1 red onion, thinly sliced
- 1 tsp garlic powder
- 1 tsp smoked paprika
- ½ tsp ground cumin
- 1 tbsp olive oil
- Low-calorie spray oil
- Fresh parsley, chopped, for garnish
- Lemon wedges, for serving
- Salt & pepper to taste

NUTRITION

- Calories: 220
- Protein: 30g
- Total Fat: 9g
- Saturated Fat: 1.5g
- Carbs: 6g
- Fibre: 2g
- Sugars: 2g

METHOD

1 In a large bowl, combine the prawns, red onion, garlic powder, smoked paprika, ground cumin, olive oil, salt, and pepper.

2 Lightly spray the prawn mixture with oil and place in the air fryer basket in a single layer, ensuring the prawns and onions are spread evenly.

3 Cook at 200°C (390°F) for 8-10 minutes, shaking the basket halfway through, until the prawns are crispy and the onions are slightly caramelized.

4 Garnish with chopped parsley and serve with lemon wedges.

FRIED SQUID RINGS

Serves 4

INGREDIENTS

- 400g squid rings
- 1 tsp smoked paprika
- ½ tsp ground cumin
- ½ tsp garlic powder
- Pinch of cayenne pepper
- 1 tbsp olive oil
- 1 lemon, cut into wedges
- 2 tbsp chopped fresh leaf parsley
- Low-calorie spray oil
- Salt & pepper to taste

NUTRITION

- Calories: 180
- Protein: 26g
- Total Fat: 7g
- Saturated Fat: 1.5g
- Carbs: 3g
- Fibre: 1g
- Sugars: 1g

METHOD

1 In a large bowl, combine the smoked paprika, ground cumin, garlic powder, cayenne pepper, olive oil, salt and pepper.

2 Lightly spray the squid rings with oil and place in the air fryer basket, ensuring they are in a single layer and not overcrowded (you may need to cook them in batches).

3 Cook at 200°C (390°F) for 6-8 minutes, shaking the basket halfway through to ensure even cooking, until the squid is tender and slightly crispy on the edges.

4 Garnish with freshly chopped parsley and serve with lemon wedges on the side.

VEGETABLES & SIDE DISHES

BALSAMIC ROASTED VEGETABLES

Serves 4

INGREDIENTS

- 1 red pepper, sliced
- 1 red onion, sliced
- 1 carrot, cut into batons
- 200g whole button mushrooms
- 200g baby corn
- 200g spinach
- 1 tbsp balsamic vinegar
- 1 tsp dried rosemary
- Low-calorie spray oil
- Salt & pepper to taste

NUTRITION

- Calories: 150
- Protein: 5g
- Total Fat: 5g
- Saturated Fat: 1g
- Carbs: 25g
- Fibre: 8g
- Sugars: 10g

METHOD

1 Place the sliced red pepper, onion, carrot batons, button mushrooms, and baby corn in an air fryer-safe dish. Lightly spray with low-calorie oil and drizzle with balsamic vinegar. Sprinkle with dried rosemary.

2 Cook at 180°C (350°F) for 15-20 minutes, or until the vegetables are tender. Add the spinach in the last 2-3 minutes of cooking to wilt.

3 Season with salt and pepper and serve.

ANCHOVY BROCCOLI WITH CHILLI

Serves 4

INGREDIENTS

- 600g tenderstem broccoli
- 1 onion, finely sliced
- ½ tsp crushed chillies
- 5 tinned anchovy fillets in olive oil (drain & reserve the oil)
- Lemon wedges to serve
- Salt & pepper to taste

NUTRITION

- Calories: 180
- Protein: 8g
- Total Fat: 7g
- Saturated Fat: 2g
- Carbs: 18g
- Fibre: 7g
- Sugars: 5g

METHOD

1 Place the broccoli, onion, chilli, anchovy fillets, and 1 tbsp of the reserved anchovy oil in an air fryer-safe dish.

2 Cook at 180°C (350°F) for 15-20 minutes, or until the broccoli is tender and cooked through.

3 Season and serve with lemon wedges.

MUSTARD POTATOES WITH SPINACH

Serves 4

INGREDIENTS

- 500g baby new potatoes, halved
- 1 tsp garlic powder
- 1 tbsp whole grain mustard
- 200g spinach, roughly chopped
- 1 tbsp lemon juice
- Low-calorie spray oil
- Salt & pepper to taste

NUTRITION

- Calories: 210
- Protein: 6g
- Total Fat: 5g
- Saturated Fat: 1g
- Carbs: 35g
- Fibre: 6g
- Sugars: 3g

METHOD

1 Place the halved new potatoes, garlic powder, and spray with low-calorie oil in an air fryer-safe dish. Cook at 180°C (350°F) for 20 minutes.

2 Add the roughly chopped spinach, drizzle with lemon juice, and stir in the whole grain mustard. Continue cooking for an additional 10-20 minutes, or until the potatoes are tender.

3 Season with salt and pepper and serve.

GINGER CABBAGE & PEAS

Serves 4

INGREDIENTS

- 1 onion, sliced
- 1 tsp ground ginger
- 1 tsp garlic powder
- 1 green cabbage, shredded
- 250g peas
- 2 tbsp water
- Low-calorie spray oil
- Salt & pepper to taste

NUTRITION

- Calories: 160
- Protein: 6g
- Total Fat: 3g
- Saturated Fat: 1g
- Carbs: 28g
- Fibre: 8g
- Sugars: 10g

METHOD

1 Place the sliced onion, ground ginger, garlic powder, and spray with low-calorie oil in an air fryer-safe dish. Cook at 180°C (350°F) for 5 minutes.

2 Add the shredded cabbage, peas, and water. Continue cooking for an additional 15-20 minutes, or until the cabbage and peas are tender.

3 Season with salt and pepper and serve.

HONEY-GLAZED BABY CARROTS

Serves 4

INGREDIENTS

- 400g baby carrots, cut lengthways
- 2 tsp olive oil or sunflower oil
- 2 tsp honey
- Salt & pepper to taste

NUTRITION

- Calories: 120
- Protein: 2g
- Total Fat: 5g
- Saturated Fat: 1g
- Carbs: 20g
- Fibre: 6g
- Sugars: 10g

METHOD

1 Place the cut baby carrots and oil in an air fryer-safe dish. Cook at 180°C (350°F) for 15-25 minutes, or until the carrots are crispy and tender.

2 Remove the carrots from the air fryer and place them in a bowl. Drizzle with honey and combine well.

3 Season with salt and pepper and serve immediately.

LEMON GARLIC GREEN BEANS

Serves 4

INGREDIENTS

- 400g green beans, trimmed
- 1 tsp garlic powder
- 1 lemon, zest and juice
- 1 tbsp olive oil
- 1 tsp dried thyme
- Low-calorie spray oil
- Salt & pepper to taste

NUTRITION

- Calories: 110
- Protein: 3g
- Total Fat: 7g
- Saturated Fat: 1g
- Carbs: 10g
- Fibre: 4g
- Sugars: 3g

METHOD

1 Place the green beans in an air fryer-safe dish. Lightly spray with low-calorie oil and toss with garlic powder, lemon zest, olive oil, and dried thyme.

2 Cook at 180°C (350°F) for 10-15 minutes, or until the green beans are tender and slightly crispy.

3 Drizzle with lemon juice, season with salt and pepper, and serve.

SPICED SWEET POTATO WEDGES

Serves 4

INGREDIENTS

- 500g sweet potatoes, cut into wedges
- 1 tsp smoked paprika
- 1 tsp ground cumin
- 1 tsp garlic powder
- 1 tbsp olive oil
- Low-calorie spray oil
- Salt & pepper to taste

NUTRITION

- Calories: 180
- Protein: 3g
- Total Fat: 6g
- Saturated Fat: 1g
- Carbs: 30g
- Fibre: 5g
- Sugars: 6g

METHOD

1 Place the sweet potato wedges in an air fryer-safe dish. Lightly spray with low-calorie oil and toss with smoked paprika, ground cumin, garlic powder, and olive oil.

2 Cook at 180°C (350°F) for 20-25 minutes, shaking the dish halfway through, until the wedges are crispy on the outside and tender on the inside.

3 Season with salt and pepper and serve.

ROASTED BEETROOT & FETA

Serves 4

INGREDIENTS

- 400g fresh beetroot, peeled and cut into wedges
- 1 tsp dried rosemary
- 1 tbsp balsamic vinegar
- 1 tbsp olive oil
- 50g feta cheese, crumbled
- Low-calorie spray oil
- Salt & pepper to taste

NUTRITION

- Calories: 200
- Protein: 6g
- Total Fat: 10g
- Saturated Fat: 4g
- Carbs: 22g
- Fibre: 6g
- Sugars: 14g

METHOD

1 Place the beetroot wedges in an air fryer-safe dish. Lightly spray with low-calorie oil and toss with dried rosemary, balsamic vinegar, and olive oil.

2 Cook at 180°C (350°F) for 20-25 minutes, or until the beetroot is tender.

3 Transfer to a serving dish and sprinkle with crumbled feta cheese. Season with salt and pepper and serve.

GARLIC BUTTER ASPARAGUS

Serves 4

INGREDIENTS

- 400g asparagus, trimmed
- 1 tsp garlic powder
- 1 tbsp unsalted butter, melted
- 1 tsp lemon juice
- Low-calorie spray oil
- Salt & pepper to taste

NUTRITION

- Calories: 100
- Protein: 3g
- Total Fat: 8g
- Saturated Fat: 4g
- Carbs: 6g
- Fibre: 3g
- Sugars: 2g

METHOD

1 Place the asparagus in an air fryer-safe dish. Lightly spray with low-calorie oil and toss with garlic powder.

2 Cook at 180°C (350°F) for 8-10 minutes, or until the asparagus is tender.

3 Drizzle with melted butter and lemon juice. Season with salt and pepper and serve.

HERB-CRUSTED CAULIFLOWER

Serves 4

INGREDIENTS

- 1 medium cauliflower, cut into florets
- 2 tbsp wholemeal breadcrumbs
- 1 tsp garlic powder
- 1 tsp dried thyme
- 1 tsp dried parsley
- 1 tbsp olive oil
- Low-calorie spray oil
- Salt & pepper to taste

NUTRITION

- Calories: 140
- Protein: 4g
- Total Fat: 7g
- Saturated Fat: 1g
- Carbs: 18g
- Fibre: 6g
- Sugars: 4g

METHOD

1 Place the cauliflower florets in an air fryer-safe dish. Lightly spray with low-calorie oil and toss with garlic powder, dried thyme, dried parsley, breadcrumbs, and olive oil.

2 Cook at 180°C (350°F) for 15-20 minutes, or until the cauliflower is golden and tender.

3 Season with salt and pepper and serve.

LEMON HERB COURGETTE

Serves 4

INGREDIENTS

- 2 medium courgettes, sliced
- 1 tbsp lemon juice
- 1 tsp dried oregano
- 1 tsp garlic powder
- Low-calorie spray oil
- Salt & pepper to taste

NUTRITION

- Calories: 23
- Protein: 0.75g
- Total Fat: 1g
- Saturated Fat: 0.25g
- Carbs: 3g
- Fibre: 1g
- Sugars: 1.25g

METHOD

1 Place the sliced courgette in an air fryer-safe dish. Lightly spray with low-calorie oil and toss with lemon juice, dried oregano, and garlic powder.

2 Cook at 180°C (350°F) for 10-15 minutes, or until the courgette is tender and slightly caramelized.

3 Season with salt and pepper and serve.

TERIYAKI TOFU & BROCCOLI

Serves 4

INGREDIENTS

- 200g firm tofu, cubed
- 300g broccoli florets
- 1 tbsp teriyaki sauce
- 1 tsp garlic powder
- Low-calorie spray oil
- Salt & pepper to taste

NUTRITION

- Calories: 55
- Protein: 4g
- Total Fat: 2.5g
- Saturated Fat: 0.5g
- Carbs: 4g
- Fibre: 1.5g
- Sugars: 1g

METHOD

1 Place the cubed tofu and broccoli florets in an air fryer-safe dish. Lightly spray with low-calorie oil and toss with garlic powder.

2 Drizzle with teriyaki sauce and cook at 180°C (350°F) for 15-20 minutes, shaking the dish halfway through, until the tofu is crispy and the broccoli is tender.

3 Season with salt and pepper and serve.

SPICY TOFU STIR-FRY

Serves 4

INGREDIENTS

- 200g firm tofu, cubed
- 1 red pepper, sliced
- 1 onion, sliced
- 200g sugar snap peas
- 1 tsp crushed chilli flakes
- 1 tbsp soy sauce
- Low-calorie spray oil
- Salt & pepper to taste

NUTRITION

- Calories: 57
- Protein: 3.25g
- Total Fat: 2.25g
- Saturated Fat: 0.5g
- Carbs: 5g
- Fibre: 1.75g
- Sugars: 2g

METHOD

1 Place the cubed tofu, pepper, onion, and sugar snap peas in an air fryer-safe dish. Lightly spray with low-calorie oil and toss with crushed red pepper flakes.

2 Drizzle with soy sauce and cook at 180°C (350°F) for 15-20 minutes, shaking the dish halfway through, until the tofu is crispy and vegetables are tender.

3 Season with salt and pepper and serve.

GARLIC ROSEMARY CHICKPEAS

Serves 4

INGREDIENTS

- 400g canned chickpeas, drained and rinsed
- 1 tsp garlic powder
- 1 tsp dried rosemary
- 1 tbsp olive oil
- Low-calorie spray oil
- Salt & pepper to taste

NUTRITION

- Calories: 105
- Protein: 3.5g
- Total Fat: 4g
- Saturated Fat: 0.5g
- Carbs: 13g
- Fibre: 3g
- Sugars: 1g

METHOD

1 Place the drained chickpeas in an air fryer-safe dish. Lightly spray with low-calorie oil and toss with garlic powder, dried rosemary, and olive oil.

2 Cook at 180°C (350°F) for 15-20 minutes, shaking the dish halfway through, until the chickpeas are crispy.

3 Season with salt and pepper and serve.

THYME ROASTED ROOT VEG

Serves 4

INGREDIENTS

- 3 medium carrots, cut into batons
- 3 medium parsnips, cut into batons
- 1 small butternut squash, peeled & cubed
- 1 red onion, cut into wedges
- 2 tbsp olive oil
- 1 lemon zest & juice
- 2 tsp dried thyme
- 1 tsp garlic powder
- Salt & pepper to taste

NUTRITION

- Calories: 200
- Protein: 3g
- Total Fat: 9g
- Saturated Fat: 1.5g
- Carbs: 30g
- Fibre: 7g
- Sugars: 10g

METHOD

1 In a large bowl, combine the carrots, parsnips, butternut squash and red onion. Add the olive oil, lemon zest, garlic powder, dried thyme, salt and pepper. Toss to coat all the vegetables evenly.

2 Place the seasoned vegetables in the air fryer basket and cook at 180°C (350°F) for 20-25 minutes, shaking the basket halfway through cooking, until the vegetables are tender and lightly browned.

3 Once cooked, transfer the vegetables to a serving dish. Drizzle with fresh lemon juice, season and serve.

WHOLEFOOD SNACKS

CINNAMON APPLE CHIPS

Serves 1

INGREDIENTS

- 2 medium apples, thinly sliced
- ½ tsp cinnamon

NUTRITION

- Calories: 160 kcal
- Protein: 0.6g
- Total Fat: 0g
- Carbohydrates: 42g
- Fibre: 8g
- Sugars: 32g

METHOD

1 Toss the apple slices with cinnamon.

2 Air fry at 160°C for 10-12 minutes, shaking halfway through, until crispy.

AIR-FRIED PINEAPPLE RINGS

Serves 1

INGREDIENTS

- 4 pineapple rings (about 200g)
- Pinch of cinnamon or chilli powder
- Low-calorie spray oil

NUTRITION

- Calories: 100 kcal
- Protein: 1g
- Total Fat: 0g
- Carbohydrates: 26g
- Fibre: 2g
- Sugars: 20g

METHOD

1 Lightly spray the pineapple rings with low-calorie oil, sprinkle with cinnamon or chilli powder.

2 Air fry at 180°C for 8-10 minutes until caramelized.

CRISPY BANANA CHIPS

Serves 1

INGREDIENTS

- 2 small bananas, peeled & thinly sliced
- Pinch of cinnamon

NUTRITION

- Calories: 180 kcal
- Protein: 2g
- Total Fat: 0g
- Carbohydrates: 46g
- Fibre: 6g
- Sugars: 24g

METHOD

1 Toss the banana slices with a pinch of cinnamon.

2 Air fry at 160°C for 8-10 minutes until crispy.

HONEY-GLAZED PEAR SLICES

Serves 1

INGREDIENTS

- 2 small pears, thinly sliced
- 1 tsp honey

NUTRITION

- Calories: 140 kcal
- Protein: 0.8g
- Total Fat: 0g
- Carbohydrates: 36g
- Fibre: 6g
- Sugars: 26g

METHOD

1 Drizzle the pear slices with honey.

2 Air fry at 180°C for 8-10 minutes until soft and caramelized.

ROASTED STRAWBERRIES

Serves 1

INGREDIENTS

- 16 strawberries, halved
- Low-calorie spray oil

NUTRITION

- Calories: 60 kcal
- Protein: 1.2g
- Total Fat: 0g
- Carbohydrates: 14g
- Fibre: 4g
- Sugars: 8g

METHOD

1 Lightly spray the strawberries with oil.

2 Air fry at 180°C for 8-10 minutes until they become slightly jammy and roasted.

SPICED PEACH HALVES

Serves 1

INGREDIENTS

- 2 medium peaches, halved and pitted
- Pinch of cinnamon or nutmeg

NUTRITION

- Calories: 120 kcal
- Protein: 2g
- Total Fat: 0g
- Carbohydrates: 30g
- Fibre: 4g
- Sugars: 26g

METHOD

1 Sprinkle the peach halves with cinnamon or nutmeg.

2 Air fry at 180°C for 10-12 minutes until tender and lightly caramelized.

BAKED GRAPEFRUIT

Serves 1

INGREDIENTS

- 1 grapefruit, halved
- 1 tsp honey or maple syrup
- Pinch of cinnamon

NUTRITION

- Calories: 100 kcal
- Protein: 1g
- Total Fat: 0g
- Carbohydrates: 24g
- Fibre: 4g
- Sugars: 18g

METHOD

1 Drizzle the grapefruit halves with honey or maple syrup, sprinkle with cinnamon.

2 Air fry at 180°C for 8-10 minutes until warm and slightly caramelized.

CRISPY KIWI CHIPS

Serves 1

INGREDIENTS

- 4 kiwis, thinly sliced
- Low-calorie spray oil

NUTRITION

- Calories: 168 kcal
- Protein: 2g
- Total Fat: 0g
- Carbohydrates: 40g
- Fibre: 8g
- Sugars: 28g

METHOD

1 Lightly spray the kiwi slices with oil.

2 Air fry at 160°C for 6-8 minutes until crispy.

AIR-FRIED MANGO SLICES

Serves 1

INGREDIENTS

- Flesh of 1 mango, sliced into strips
- Low-calorie spray oil

NUTRITION

- Calories: 150-160 kcal
- Protein: 1g
- Total Fat: 0g
- Carbohydrates: 40g
- Fibre: 3g
- Sugars: 34g

METHOD

1 Lightly spray the mango slices with oil.

2 Air fry at 180°C for 6-8 minutes until golden and slightly crispy.

CARAMELIZED PLUMS

Serves 1

INGREDIENTS

- 4 small plums, halved and pitted
- Low-calorie spray oil

NUTRITION

- Calories: 100 kcal
- Protein: 1g
- Total Fat: 0g
- Carbohydrates: 24g
- Fibre: 4g
- Sugars: 20g

METHOD

1 Lightly spray the plum halves with oil.

2 Air fry at 180°C for 8-10 minutes until soft and caramelized.

CRISPY KALE CHIPS

Serves 1

INGREDIENTS

- 100g kale, stems removed and leaves torn into pieces
- ½ tsp garlic powder
- Salt, to taste
- Low-calorie spray oil

NUTRITION

- Calories: 60 kcal
- Protein: 3g
- Total Fat: 1.5g
- Carbohydrates: 9g
- Fibre: 4g
- Sugars: 1g

METHOD

1 Toss the kale with garlic powder and salt.

2 Lightly spray with low-calorie spray oil and air fry at 150°C for 5-7 minutes, shaking halfway through, until crispy.

SWEET POTATO FRIES

Serves 1

INGREDIENTS

- 1 medium sweet potato, cut into thin fries
- ½ tsp smoked paprika
- Salt, to taste
- Low-calorie spray oil

NUTRITION

- Calories: 120 kcal
- Protein: 2g
- Total Fat: 1.5g
- Carbohydrates: 28g
- Fibre: 4g
- Sugars: 6g

METHOD

1 Toss the sweet potato fries with smoked paprika and salt.

2 Lightly spray with low-calorie spray oil and air fry at 200°C for 12-15 minutes, shaking halfway through, until crispy.

COURGETTE CHIPS

Serves 1

INGREDIENTS

- 1 medium courgette, sliced into thin rounds
- ½ tsp dried oregano
- Salt & pepper, to taste
- Low-calorie spray oil

NUTRITION

- Calories: 50 kcal
- Protein: 2g
- Total Fat: 1.5g
- Carbohydrates: 10g
- Fibre: 2g
- Sugars: 4g

METHOD

1 Toss the courgette slices with oregano, salt, and pepper.

2 Lightly spray with low-calorie spray oil and air fry at 180°C for 10-12 minutes, shaking halfway through, until crispy.

PARSNIP CRISPS

Serves 1

INGREDIENTS

- 1 medium parsnip, peeled and thinly sliced
- ½ tsp ground cumin
- Salt, to taste
- Low-calorie spray oil

NUTRITION

- Calories: 80 kcal
- Protein: 1g
- Total Fat: 1.5g
- Carbohydrates: 18g
- Fibre: 5g
- Sugars: 4g

METHOD

1 Toss the parsnip slices with cumin and salt.

2 Lightly spray with low-calorie spray oil and air fry at 180°C for 10-12 minutes, shaking halfway through, until crispy.

SPICED CARROT FRIES

Serves 1

INGREDIENTS

- 2 medium carrots, cut into thin fries
- ½ tsp ground coriander
- ½ tsp ground paprika
- Salt, to taste
- Low-calorie spray oil

NUTRITION

- Calories: 60 kcal
- Protein: 1g
- Total Fat: 1.5g
- Carbohydrates: 14g
- Fibre: 4g
- Sugars: 7g

METHOD

1 Toss the carrot fries with coriander, paprika, and salt.

2 Lightly spray with low-calorie spray oil and air fry at 200°C for 10-12 minutes, shaking halfway through, until crispy.

BUTTERNUT SQUASH BITES

Serves 1

INGREDIENTS

- 200g butternut squash, peeled and cut into cubes
- ½ tsp cinnamon or smoked paprika (optional)
- Salt, to taste
- Low-calorie spray oil

NUTRITION

- Calories: 80 kcal
- Protein: 1g
- Total Fat: 1.5g
- Carbohydrates: 21g
- Fibre: 3g
- Sugars: 4g

METHOD

1 Toss the butternut squash cubes with cinnamon or smoked paprika and salt.

2 Lightly spray with low-calorie spray oil and air fry at 200°C for 12-15 minutes, shaking halfway through, until tender and golden.

SPICY CHICKPEAS

Serves 1

INGREDIENTS

- 100g canned chickpeas, drained and rinsed
- ½ tsp chilli powder
- ½ tsp cumin
- Salt, to taste
- Low-calorie spray oil

NUTRITION

- Calories: 160 kcal
- Protein: 6g
- Total Fat: 3g
- Carbohydrates: 25g
- Fibre: 7g
- Sugars: 2g

METHOD

1 Toss the chickpeas with chilli powder, cumin, and salt.

2 Lightly spray with low-calorie spray oil and air fry at 200°C for 10-12 minutes, shaking halfway through, until crispy.

GARLIC MUSHROOMS

Serves 1

INGREDIENTS

- 150g button mushrooms, halved
- 1 tsp garlic powder
- Salt & pepper, to taste
- Low-calorie spray oil

NUTRITION

- Calories: 50 kcal
- Protein: 4g
- Total Fat: 1.5g
- Carbohydrates: 7g
- Fibre: 2g
- Sugars: 2g

METHOD

1 Toss the mushrooms with garlic powder, salt, and pepper.

2 Lightly spray with low-calorie spray oil and air fry at 180°C for 8-10 minutes, shaking halfway through, until golden and tender.

BRUSSELS SPROUTS CHIPS

Serves 1

INGREDIENTS

- 150g Brussels sprouts, trimmed and halved
- ½ tsp garlic powder
- Salt & pepper, to taste
- Low-calorie spray oil

NUTRITION

- Calories: 60 kcal
- Protein: 4g
- Total Fat: 1.5g
- Carbohydrates: 12g
- Fibre: 5g
- Sugars: 2g

METHOD

1 Toss the Brussels sprouts with garlic powder, salt, and pepper.

2 Lightly spray with low-calorie spray oil and air fry at 180°C for 10-12 minutes, shaking halfway through, until crispy on the edges.

BROCCOLI BITES

Serves 1

INGREDIENTS

- 150g broccoli florets
- 2 tsp grated Parmesan cheese
- Salt & pepper, to taste
- Low-calorie spray oil

NUTRITION

- Calories: 110 kcal
- Protein: 8g
- Total Fat: 4g
- Carbohydrates:10g
- Fibre: 4g
- Sugars: 2g

METHOD

1 Toss the broccoli florets with Parmesan, salt, and pepper.

2 Lightly spray with low-calorie spray oil and air fry at 180°C for 8-10 minutes, shaking halfway through, until tender and slightly crispy.